Contents

MW00568048

Encouraging Interest

Help students to develop an understanding and appreciation for different artists and types of art by highlighting a variety of artists each month. Display examples of an artist's work and have students study and duplicate the style. In addition, encourage students to visit art museums online or visit local art galleries.

Student Art Portfolios

Give each student a large sketchbook in which to explore art techniques, create designs, collect examples of artwork they admire and challenge their thinking about art. Encourage students to add to their art portfolios at least once a week.

Colouring Pages

These pages are intended to give students practice in using different elements of design.

Rubrics and Checklists

Use the rubrics in this book to assess student learning.

Learning Logs

In addition to an art portfolio, have students keep a learning log as an effective way to organize their thoughts and ideas about art concepts presented. Learning logs can include the following kinds of entries:

- teacher journal prompts
- student personal reflections
- questions that arise
- connections discovered
- labelled diagrams

Art Glossary

List new art vocabulary and meanings on chart paper for students' reference during activities.

Teacher Tips 2

Tracing and Cutting Practice 5

Elements of Design:
Colour Activities 7

Elements of Design:
Line Activities 18

Elements of Design:
Form Activities 23

Elements of Design:
Texture Activities 39

Elements of Design:
Shape Activities 42

Colouring Fun 51

Create, Design, Draw 59

Direct Draw 63

Sketchbook and Collage Ideas 64

Seasonal Activity Ideas 65

Seasonal Colouring Fun 69

Art Rubrics 73

Art Websites for Students 76

Art Glossary 77

Student Art Certificates 80

Teacher Tips

Art Centre Organization

- Keep materials for individual art centres in separate bins so that the activity is easily accessible. In addition, make sure there are enough materials for each student, along with an artwork sample of what is expected.
- Introduce and explain the expectation of each learning centre to students. Model and reinforce skills needed to complete an art activity.
- Provide free exploration art centres such as:
  - **Sculpture-making** where students can experiment with different types of playdough
  - **Printmaking** where students can experiment producing different rubbings or print transfers using a variety of materials
  - **Mixed media** where students can choose and plan their own piece of artwork using found materials
  - **Paint centre** where students can experiment using different types of textured paints to produce a picture
  - **Observational drawing centre** where students can practise sketching various objects and arrangements
  - **Building centre** where students can explore creating structures using different types of building toys, as well as found materials such as corks, caps, tubes, etc.
  - **Paper doll-making centre** where students can create their own paper dolls with different features and outfits. Provide different materials such as scissors, paper doll outlines, different papers, yarn, wiggle eyes, paint, tissue paper, wrapping paper, felt and colouring materials.
  - **Lacing centre** where students can hole punch different designs on the shape outlines provided and then lace with different colours of yarn.

Routines

Establish clear expectations and responsibilities of students while at each centre and the number of students allowed per centre. Also, make sure students are involved in cleanup and know where to put away materials. The teacher may wish to ring a bell or play music to signal when it is time to move to a different centre or to clean up.

Other Teacher Tips

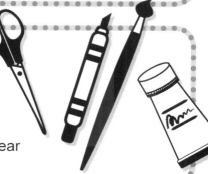

- Validate student art and encourage students to take their time.
- Provide plenty of time to finish artwork.
- Display student artwork and celebrate it.
- Encourage students to experiment and explore different media.
- Ask parents or guardians to send in old shirts that students can wear when completing art activities.

Teacher Tips

Colouring Skills

- Demonstrate for students how by applying different pressure when colouring with a crayon or pencil crayon a deeper or lighter colour will result. Also, point out and demonstrate how using heavy pressure to create a deeper colour for an object or area of a composition is a good way to make the object or area visually stand out.
- Model for students how to take their time and colour within the lines. Techniques include colouring in the same direction, and first outlining the area to be coloured.
- Encourage students to use black or dark crayon colours to outline shapes and objects while colouring to make them easier to see from a distance.

Painting Skills

- Model and reinforce for students how to place paint on the paintbrush so that there isn't too much paint.
- Demonstrate for students how to take their time when painting so they can control where the paint falls and they can vary the size and type of stroke.
- Remind students to clean their brush each time they switch colours.

Pasting Skills

- Model for students how to apply small amounts of glue or paste around the edges of the art project so that glue does not overflow.
- Model for students the importance of applying pressure upon the glued or pasted area so that the glue sticks appropriately.
- Demonstrate for students different ways of applying glue or paste using fingers, toothpicks, tongue depressors or a squirt bottle.

Cutting Skills

- Always carefully and directly supervise students when they are using scissors.
- Model and reinforce with students how to hold scissors correctly. Also, demonstrate how to safely hand over scissors to others.
- During cutting activities be sure to encourage students to cut with "thumbs up." Discourage students from holding their thumb toward the floor while cutting.
- Demonstrate and reinforce with students how to turn paper to adapt to the scissors as they cut.

Tearing Skills

- Model for students how tearing paper is a controlled action where they need to take their time.

Crazy Colouring Ideas

Students can practise their fine motor skills by using different media to colour or to fill in sections of a colouring page or simple geometric shapes.

Have students try colouring:

- on different surfaces, such as sandpaper, to create interesting textures
- by alternating heavy and light strokes with crayons or pencil crayons
- using only primary colours
- using only secondary colours
- using only shades of grey
- using warm colours
- using cool colours
- using different tints and shades of one colour
- with chalk or oil pastels and setting the colouring page with hairspray

Have students fill in sections of a colouring page or large geometric shapes using:

- watercolours
- tempera paint
- different types of lines such as vertical, horizontal, wavy, etc.
- patterns
- different textured paints and finishes
- different colours of Plasticine
- tiny bits of torn construction paper
- tissue paper squares
- seeds
- fingerpainting techniques
- mixed media
- different colours of thick yarn
- cotton swab or marker dots

Trace and cut along the lines.

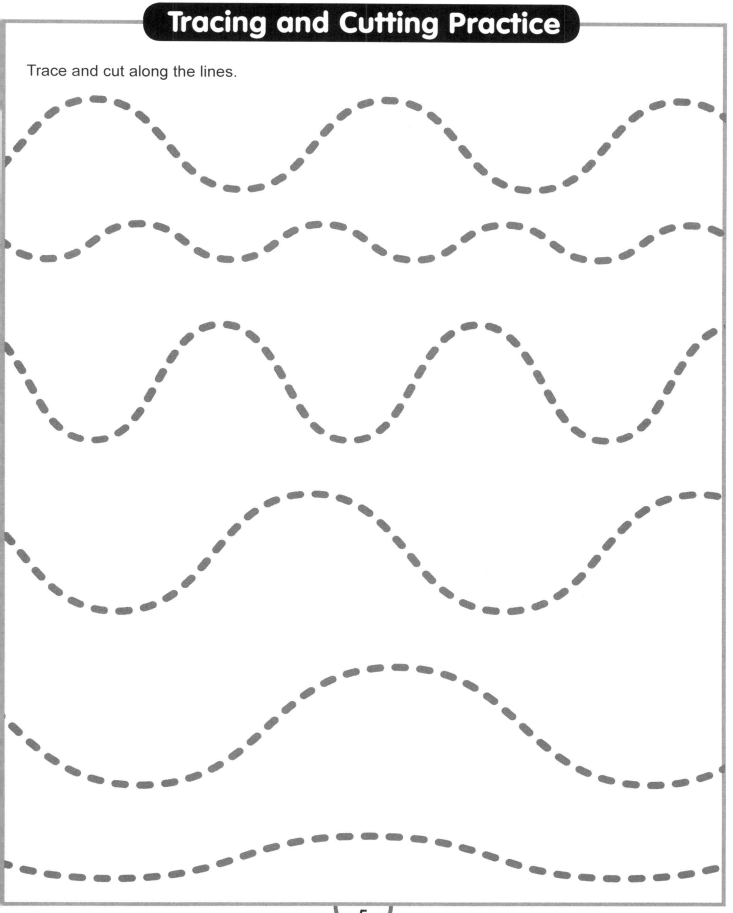

Trace and cut along the lines.

Elements Of Design: Colour

Activity 1: Primary and Secondary Colour String Prints

What you need:

- Tempera paint in the primary colours
- Styrofoam plates to hold paint for dipping
- White paper
- White yarn

What to do:

1. Have students carefully dip yarn into red paint and then slide the yarn across the white paper.
2. Next, repeat the process with yellow paint. As the yellow paint overlaps and crosses the red paint, the colour orange will result. Discuss with students what they see. Reinforce the art terms *primary colours* and *secondary colours*.
3. Then, repeat the process with the blue paint. Have students point out different colours that result as paint colours overlap and cross each other.

Activity 2: Colour Day

Designate a certain day to a particular colour, for example "Red Day." Encourage students to come to school wearing a particular colour, and to bring pictures or items in that colour. Then, have students notice and classify varying shades of the designated colour. You may also wish to create a class collage of pictures, wallpaper, wrapping paper, yarn, etc., in the designated colour.

Activity 3: Fingerpainting with One Colour

What you need:

- Fingerpaint of one colour in different tints or shades
- White paper
- Styrofoam plates

What to do:

1. While preparing paint for the centre, demonstrate for students how tints of a colour are created by adding white, and shades of a colour are created by adding black.
2. Then have students explore tints and shades by creating a fingerpainting.

Chalkboard Publishing © 2012

The Colour Wheel

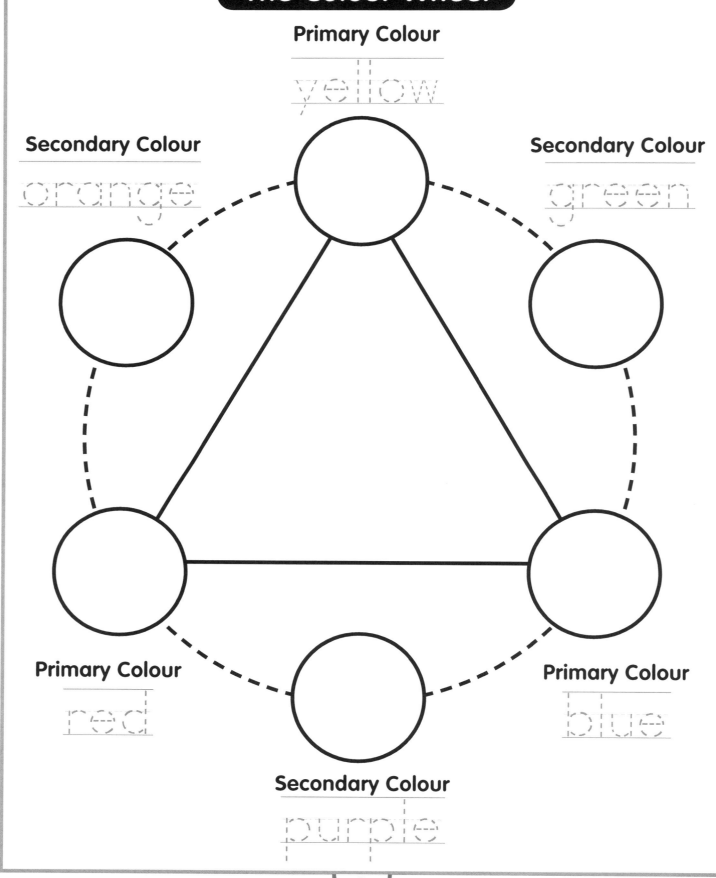

Primary Colour
yellow

Secondary Colour
orange

Secondary Colour
green

Primary Colour
red

Primary Colour
blue

Secondary Colour
purple

PRIMARY COLOURS:

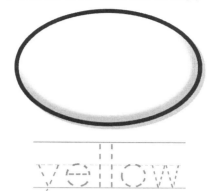  

yellow   red   blue

SECONDARY COLOURS:

 +  =

yellow   red   orange

 + =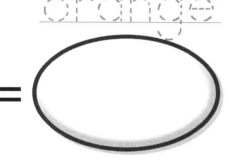

red   blue   purple

 + =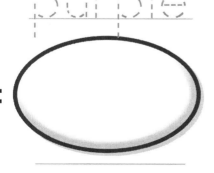

yellow   blue   green

Primary Colours

Colour the balloons using only primary colours.
The primary colours are RED, YELLOW and BLUE.

Primary Colour Collage

Look inside magazines and find, cut and paste pictures that have primary colours.

Look inside magazines and find, cut and paste pictures that have secondary colours.

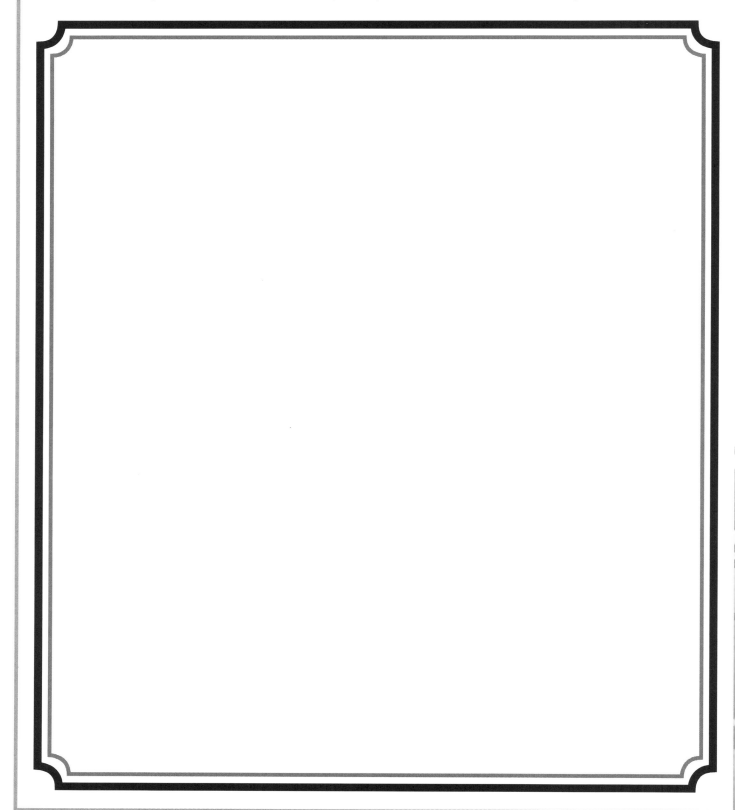

Secondary Colours

Colour the caterpillar using only secondary colours. The secondary colours are GREEN, PURPLE and ORANGE.

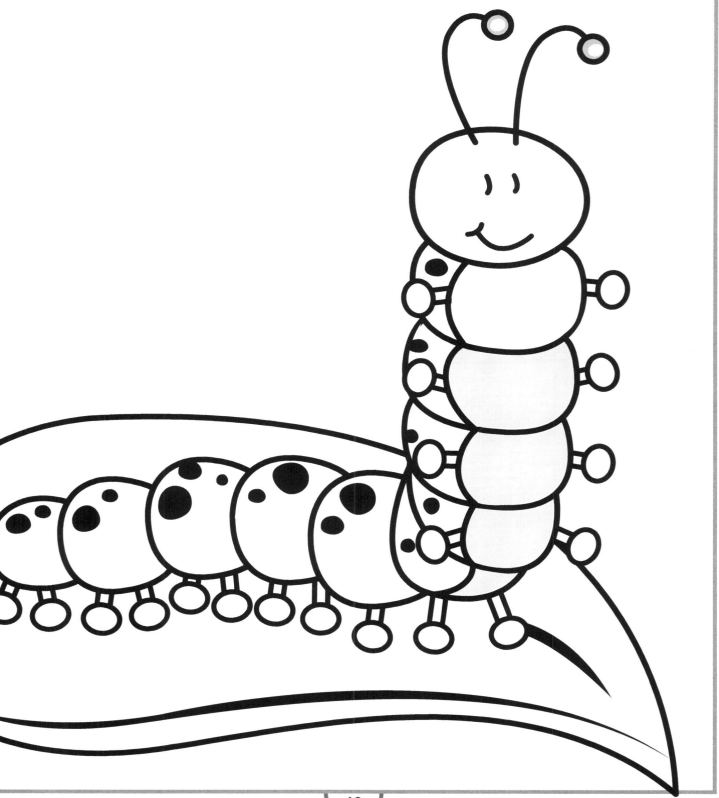

brown   blue   green

black   red   orange

purple   yellow   pink

Colour the rainbow.

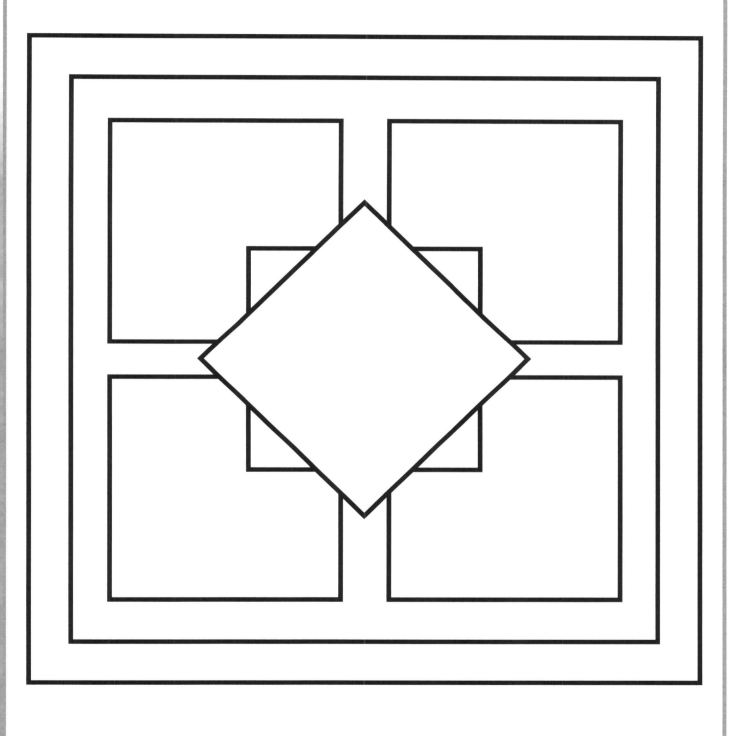

Elements Of Design: Line

Activity 1: Rhythm and Line

What you need:

- Crayons
- Pastels
- Different types of music
- Paper
- Chalk
- Pencil crayons

What to do:

1. Choose and play a piece of music for students and have them follow the rhythm of the music with a finger in the air.
2. Next, have students follow the rhythm of the music by choosing a colouring material and drawing a line across a sheet of paper.
3. Encourage the students to follow that line exactly with other lines above and below the first line, changing the colours and properties of the line. For example: thick, wavy, broken, etc.
4. Repeat the activity with different types of music and discuss as a class why students chose to produce different types of lines and chose certain colours.

Activity 2: Sgraffito

What you need:

- Smooth-surfaced paper
- Crayons
- Thick tempera paint
- Paint brushes
- Objects that scratch, such as toothpicks, tongue depressors, combs, coins and plastic utensils

What to do:

1. Ask students to draw broad bands of colour using crayons on a piece of smooth-surfaced paper. Remind students to apply pressure on the crayons as they draw.
2. Once completed, have students paint over the entire paper with the black tempera paint.
3. After the paint dries, encourage students to scratch designs onto the paper using the objects. This technique is called sgraffito.

Activity 3: Loopy Line Design

What you need:

- Paper
- Crayons

What to do:

1. Model for students how to draw a design of loop shapes on a piece of paper.
2. Next, demonstrate for students how to lightly colour in each shape with different colours of crayon. Remind students to take their time and to work on staying inside the lines.
3. Then, show students how to fill in sections of each loop shape with different types of lines using black crayon.

Lines, Lines, Lines

Fill in each section with the correct type of line. Use different coloured pencils, markers or crayons. Then cut out the sections and paste them into an arrangement on a separate piece of paper.

Thin Lines ————————————————

Thick Lines ▬▬▬▬▬▬▬▬▬

Broken Lines —— —— —— —— ——

Wavy Lines ⌒⌒⌒⌒⌒

Curvy Lines ∿∿∿∿∿∿∿

Fill in each section with the correct type of line. Use different coloured pencils, markers or crayons. Then cut out the sections and paste them into an arrangement on a separate piece of paper.

Dotted Lines • • • • • • • • • • • • • • • • •

Zigzag Lines

Horizontal Lines

Vertical Lines | | | | | | | | | | | |

Diagonal Lines ///////////

Draw the other half of the picture. Colour the picture once complete.

Decorate and colour the T-shirt with an interesting pattern.

Elements Of Design: Form

Activity 1: Class Town

What you need:

- Cereal boxes, milk cartons, paper tubes
- Construction paper
- Colouring materials
- Coloured tissue paper
- Scissors
- Tape and glue
- Tempera paint mixed with liquid detergent

What to do:

1. Brainstorm a class list of buildings and areas found in your community.
2. Use different boxes as the base for various buildings in the community.
3. Decorate the buildings with construction paper, foil, paint, etc.
4. Set up the buildings together on a large table or the floor.
5. Model for students how to add construction paper strips for streets and use other scrap materials to make trees, telephone poles, etc.

Activity 2: Paper Sculpture

What you need:

- Coloured card stock or heavy construction paper • Scissors

What to do:

1. Model for students how to cut free-form shapes in different colours from the construction paper.
2. Next, demonstrate how to cut four large slits into the sides of each shape.
3. Then, show students how to a build a sculpture by interlocking the shape pieces along the slits.

Activity 3: All About Me 3D Collage Cube

What you need:

- Cube blackline master • Magazine pictures • Scissors and glue

What to do:

1. Model for students and help them to cut out and paste the blackline master into a cube.
2. Then, have students cut out magazine pictures of their favourite things to paste onto each side of the cube. For example, each side can have a theme such as favourite animals, favourite foods, favourite colour, favourite places, etc. Alternatively, students can draw pictures on each side of the cube to show their favourite things.

23

Chalkboard Publishing © 2012

Sculpture Fun

Give students opportunities to sculpt and paint different forms. Provide students with cookie cutter shapes, rollers, plastic knives, plastic spoons, and wooden craft sticks for modelling as well as colouring and paint media. Demonstrate for students how to roll, flatten, and pinch the dough to form shapes. You may also wish to provide students with wiggle eyes, buttons and piper cleaners to add to sculptures. Store dough in a sealed container.

Self-Hardening Dough

- 1 1/2 cups water
- 1 1/2 cups salt
- 4 cups flour
- 1 teaspoon alum

1. Mix dry ingredients in a bowl.
2. Gradually add water.
3. Knead until the mixture is pliable.

Sand Sculpture Dough

- 4 cups clean sand (not beach sand)
- 2 cups cornstarch
- 2 cups water

1. First, mix all ingredients for one batch of dough in a saucepan.
2. Heat the mixture over medium heat, and stir until the mixture becomes a thick consistency.
3. Once the mixture is the right consistency, allow the sand sculpture dough to cool before handling.

Smelly Modelling Dough

- 3 cups flour
- 1/2 cup salt
- 2 packages flavoured drink crystals
- 2 cups boiling water

1. Mix dry ingredients in a bowl.
2. Add boiling water.
3. Mix and knead on a floured surface.

How to Draw a Sheep

Step 1

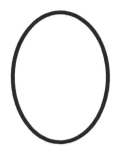

Step 2

Step 3

Step 4

Step 5

25

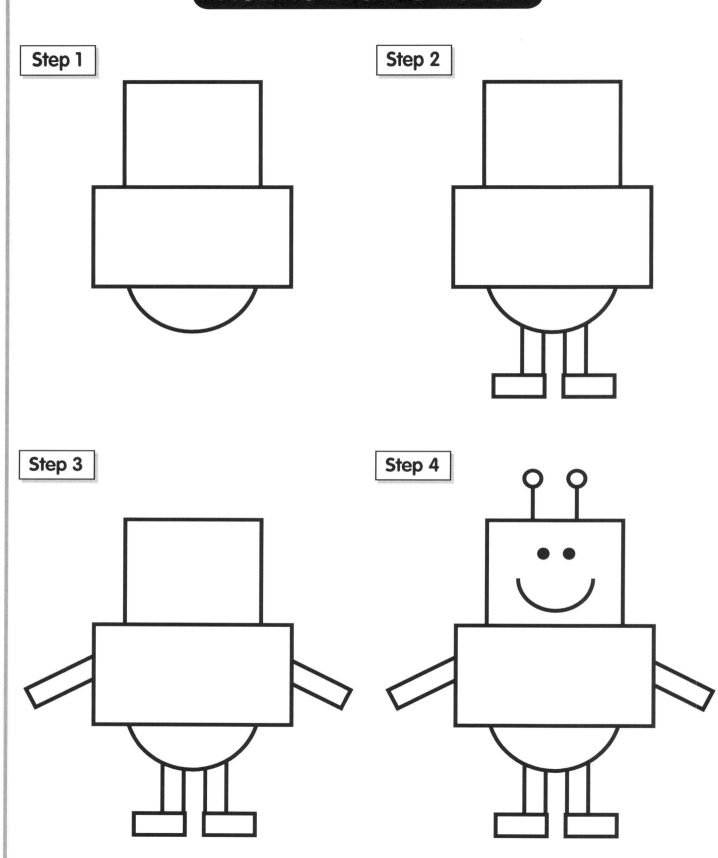

Step 1

Step 2

Step 3

Step 4

How to Draw a Bee

Step 1

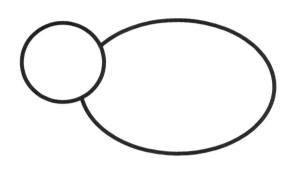

Step 2

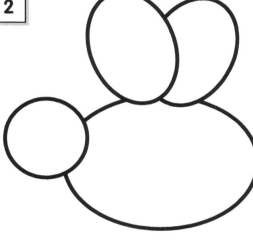

Step 3

Step 4

Step 5

How to Draw a Dog

Step 1

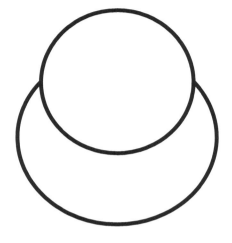

Step 2

Step 3

Step 4

How to Draw a Cat

Step 1

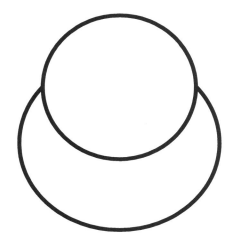

Step 2

Step 3

Step 4

How to Draw a Fish

Step 1

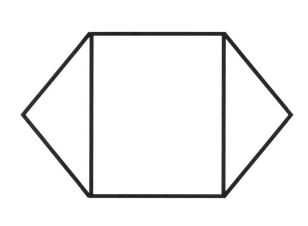

Step 2

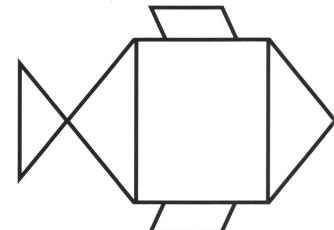

Step 3

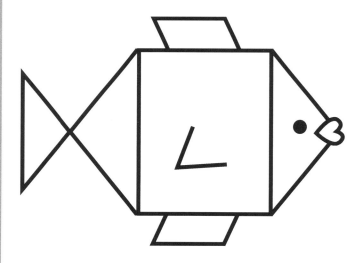

Step 4

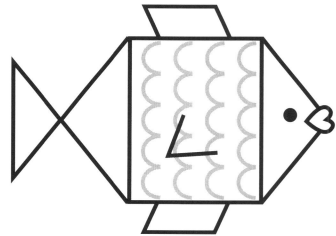

How to Draw a Spaceship

How to Draw a Plane

Step 1

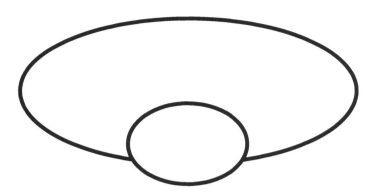

Step 2

Step 3

How to Draw a Bird

Step 1

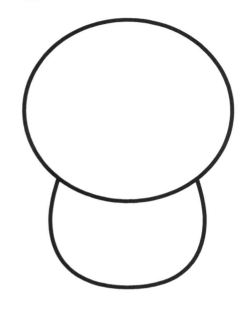

Step 2

Step 3

Step 4

How to Draw a Boat

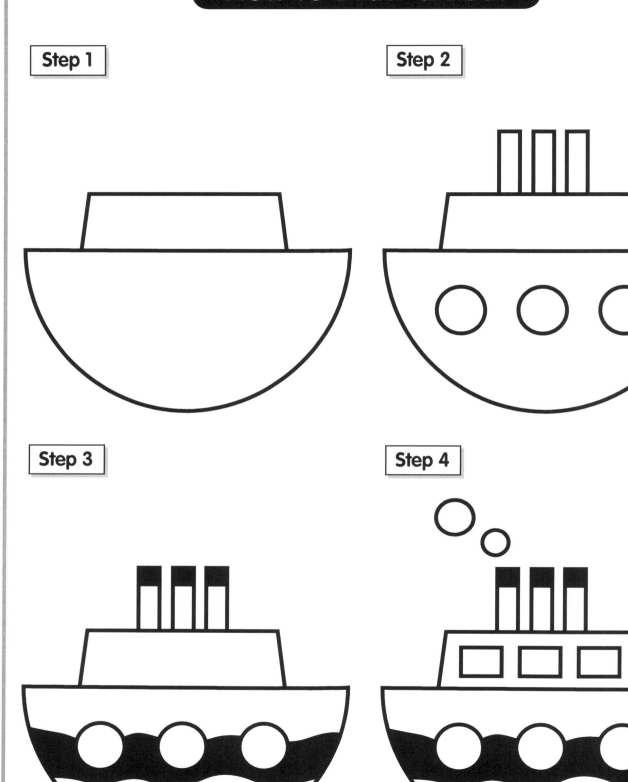

Paper Doll Outline

Cube Outline

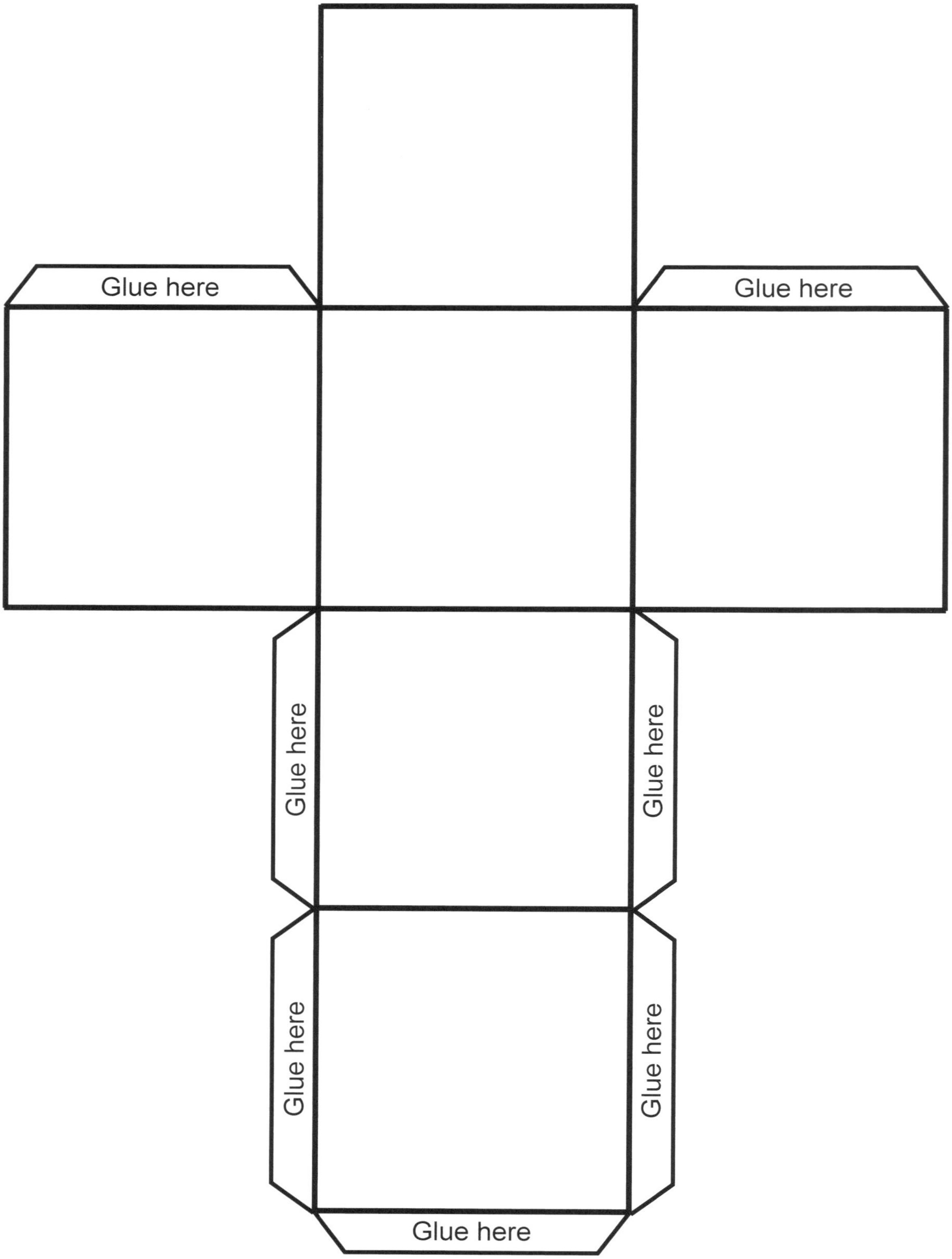

Glue here

Glue here

Glue here

Glue here

Glue here

Glue here

Glue here

Elements Of Design: Texture

Activity 1: Fruit and Veggie Printmaking

What you need:

- Cut sections of a variety of fruit and vegetables
- Styrofoam plates
- Tempera paint in assorted colours
- Paper

What to do:

1. Demonstrate for students how to carefully press cut sections of vegetables or fruit onto a Styrofoam plate with tempera paint.
2. Then show students how to press the painted section of the vegetable or fruit onto the paper to create a print.
3. Remind students not to drag vegetables or fruit across the page.
4. Encourage students to experiment with the print they make by creating patterns or other arrangements.
5. Discuss with students what vegetables or fruit they thought produced the best prints.

Activity 2: Monoprints

What you need:

- Printmaking ink or tempera paint with flour added to make the consistency thicker
- Paintbrushes
- Small sheets of Plexiglas
- Paper
- A covered work area

What to do:

1. Discuss with students that monoprinting is a process whereby only one print is pulled from the printing plate.
2. Demonstrate for students how to use their paintbrush to paint a design or picture onto the Plexiglas. Make sure to remind students that they need to work quickly so that the paint won't dry.
3. Next, show students how to place the paper over the Plexiglas and press lightly with the palm of the hand so that the design transfers onto the paper.
4. Lastly, peel away the paper and admire the monoprint.

Experiment with Texture

Encourage students to create different textures with the following ideas. Students may wish to paint several papers in a variety of colours, using the various ideas below, and then use the papers to create collages or to fill sections of a picture.

Out-of-the-Ordinary Painting Tools

- Fingers
- Sticks
- Blocks of wood
- Branches
- Rope
- Feathers
- Leaves
- Sponges
- Tissues
- Brushes
- Cotton swabs
- Cotton balls
- Plastic pot scrubbers
- Plastic wrap
- Makeup brushes

Excellent Drawing and Painting Materials

- Crayons
- Pencils
- Pastels
- Chalk
- Charcoal
- Ink pen
- Water-based markers
- Acrylic paint
- Makeup
- Tempera paint
- Felt tip pens
- Pencil crayons
- Watercolours
- Food colouring

A Variety of Surfaces on Which to Paint or Draw

- Newsprint
- Paper plates
- Blocks of wood
- Tissue paper
- Paper bags
- Sandpaper
- Wet paper
- Cardboard
- Fabric
- Plastic wrap
- Paper towels
- Waxed paper
- Aluminum foil
- Stones
- Foam

Create Different Textures

Corn Syrup Paint

Make a striking paint with an interesting texture by combining food colouring and light corn syrup. Mix up as many colours as needed. Encourage students to paint different landscapes or oceanscapes. Students may also wish to first create an outline drawing with a permanent marker before painting. Be sure to allow more than a day for drying time.

Flour-and-Water Fingerpaint

Fingerpaint is a great way to achieve different textures using fingers. Mix 1 cup flour, 1 cup water and 2 teaspoons salt in a small container to make fingerpaint with the consistency of thick gravy. Add the desired food colouring. Repeat the process for as many colours as needed.

Glossy Paint

Give tempera paint a wet glossy look by combining 1 part white glue and 1 part tempera paint.

Puff Paint

Have students create unique pictures using puff paint. Combine 1 cup salt, 1 cup sugar and the desired food colouring in a squeeze bottle. Shake the ingredients and squeeze the paint out of the bottle onto the paper.

Sand Paint

Sand paint offers an interesting option when striving to create texture in a picture. Begin by having students create a simple outline drawing. Then make the sand paint by combining 1 part sand and 5 parts powdered tempera. Encourage students to experiment when mixing the sand and tempera to reach the desired colour. Next, when a few sand paint colours have been made, use a wooden craft stick to spread a thin layer of glue in one section of the outline drawing. Then, using a spoon, gently pour the sand paint into the glued section. Lightly lift the paper to shake off any excess sand paint. Allow the sand painting to dry, and seal it using hairspray.

Wax Resist

As wax and water don't mix, the wax resist technique can be used to mask out areas to preserve the white of the paper or the colour beneath, and to create appealing textures. Draw or colour with a wax crayon and then wash over it with a water-based paint.

Elements Of Design: Shape

Activity 1: Shape Picture

What you need:

• Black construction paper • Scissors • Shape outlines • Glue • Colouring materials

What to do:

1. Ask students to plan and compose a picture based on their choice of the shape cutouts.
2. Some ideas for pictures include animals, buildings, nature, inventions or people.
3. Once students have planned a detailed composition, have students glue the shapes onto the black construction paper.
4. Encourage students to use specific colour schemes and offer different media for students to use for colouring.
5. Encourage students to overlap the shapes when creating their design. In addition, you may wish to demonstrate some ways to use the shapes, for example:

> heart—animal's feet, scales, wings, nose
> circle—wheels, head, sun, eyes, nose
> rectangle—buildings, legs, body, robot
> oval—torso, body parts, eyes, tail
> triangle—beak, fin, scales, ears, roof

Activity 2: Shape Collage

What you need:

• Paper
• Watercolours
• Paintbrushes
• Rulers
• Black markers
• Pencils

What to do:

1. Instruct students to produce a design of black outlines of overlapping geometric shapes. Encourage students to draw a variety of geometric shapes.
2. Next, have students paint in the sections of the design with a specific approach such as warm colours, cool colours, experimenting with tints, etc.
3. When students have finished, discuss with them their approach to their artwork.

Chalkboard Publishing © 2012

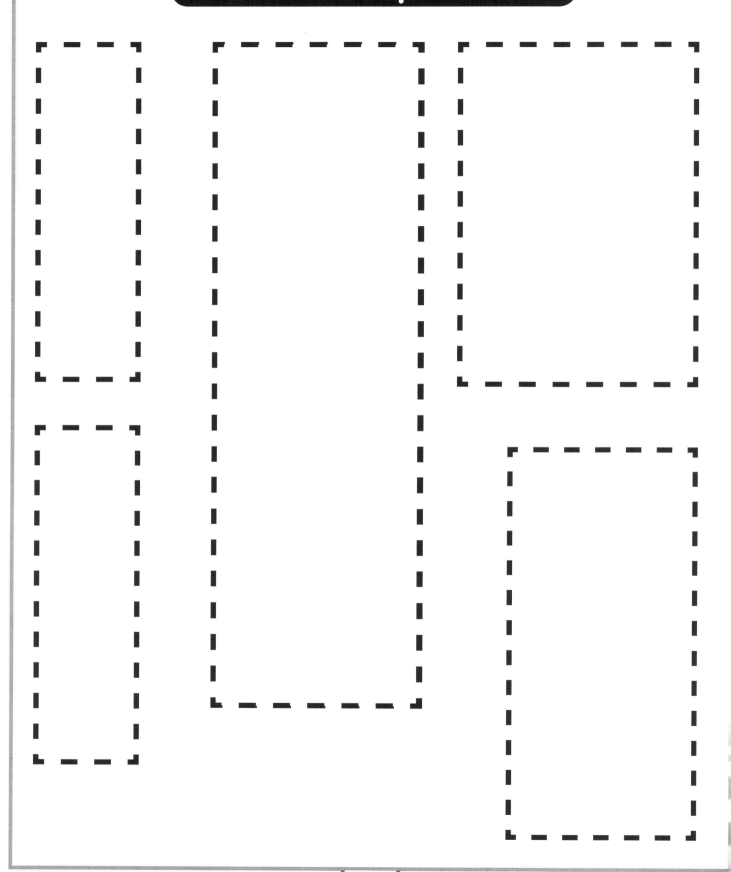

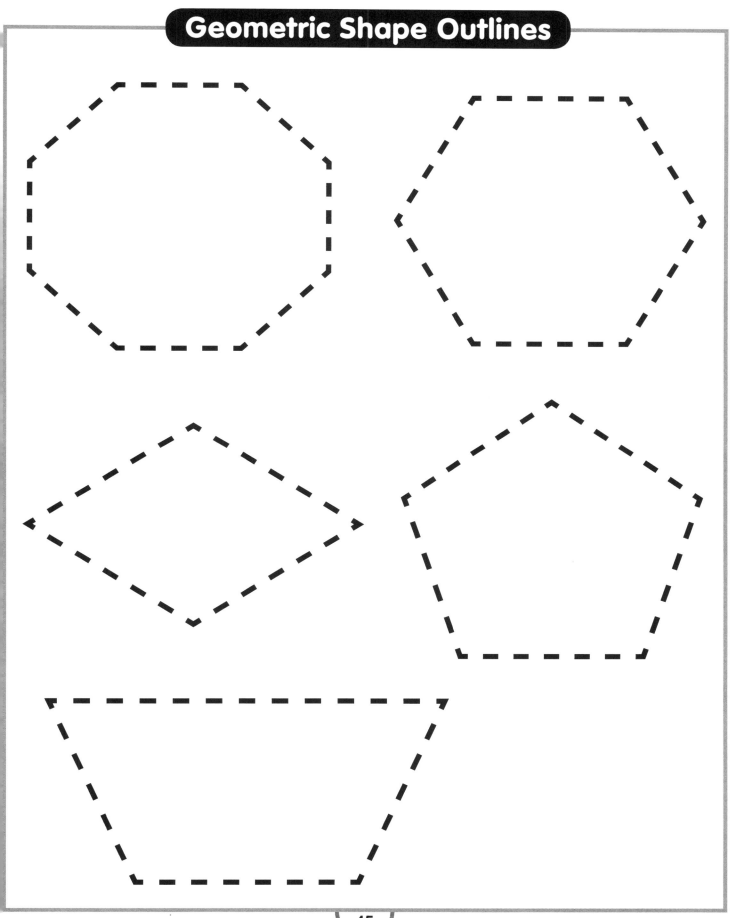

Exploring Organic Shapes: Handprint Art Ideas

Class Friendship Tree

What you need:

- Pencil and eraser
- Colouring materials
- Brown, red, orange and yellow construction paper

What to do:

1. Model for students how to trace each of their hands. Trace one hand on either red, orange or yellow construction paper to be used as a leaf. Trace the other hand on brown construction paper to be used as part of the trunk.
2. Next, ask students to print their name on their red, orange, or yellow leaf and decorate it.
3. Collect the brown construction paper hands and arrange them on a bulletin board in the form of a tree trunk and branches.
4. Then, invite students to come up to the bulletin board and add their leaves to the tree.

Handprint Butterfly

What you need:

- Pencil and eraser
- Large oval outline
- Small oval outline
- Colouring materials
- Glue and scissors
- Pipe cleaner
- Construction paper in various colours
- Decorations

What to do:

1. First, model for students how to trace and then cut out each of their hands on three pieces of different coloured construction paper. These hands will be used as the wings for the butterfly.
2. Next, have students cut out a large oval shape for the body and a small oval shape for the butterfly's head. Glue the head on top of the body.
3. Then, demonstrate for students how to arrange three butterfly wings on either side of the body so that the fingers of the hands point outward, and glue them in place.
4. Students may use marker to draw in eyes and a mouth, and then attach two pipe cleaners for the antennae.
5. Lastly, provide students with a variety of materials to decorate the butterfly wings.

Create a stamp.

Write about your stamp:

_____

- -

_____

NOSE

EYES

HAIR

MOUTH

Draw a portrait of a family member, friend or pet.

Direct Draw

Encourage students to think of art as the personal interpretation of ideas. This quick activity demonstrates how students given the same directions will each produce a unique artwork. Collect and display all of the students' completed artworks. You will have a wonderful collection of abstract art based on shape, colour and line.

WHAT YOU NEED:

- Square piece of paper
- Colouring materials

WHAT TO DO:

1. Tell students that they will each complete a piece of art by following your oral directions. Before you begin, ask students to predict whether or not all the students' works will look the same.

2. Give each student the same materials.

3. Call out directions. For example:

   - Draw a thin line across the page.

   - Draw a thick line across the page.

   - Draw a circle anywhere on the page.

   - Draw a triangle somewhere on the page.

   - ...

   Add directions of your choice that will reinforce art vocabulary. Give students enough time to follow each direction before calling out the next one.

4. When all the directions have been called out, have students compare and contrast their artworks with a partner. How are the pieces the same? How are they different?

5. Display the students' artworks.

 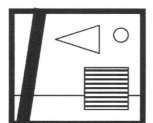 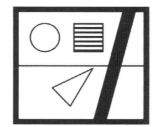 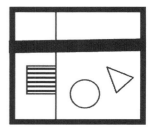

Sketchbook and Collage Ideas

Portrait

- Draw a self-portrait. Look at yourself in a mirror and add details to your portrait.
- Draw a self-portrait of yourself as a grownup.
- Draw a portrait of a friend or family member.
- Draw a portrait of your favourite stuffed animal.
- Draw a portrait of your pet.
- Draw a portrait of your favourite cartoon character.
- Draw a portrait of your teacher.
- Draw a portrait of your family.
- Draw a portrait of a grandparent.

Still Life

- Draw a beautiful flower arrangement.
- Draw a plant.
- Draw a piece of fruit.
- Draw a favourite toy.
- Draw a bowl of fruit.

Design

- Design a new cover for a book.
- Design an invitation to your birthday party.
- Design a house.
- Design a new invention.
- Design a new Canadian stamp.
- Design a new Canadian coin.
- Design a new outfit.
- Design a car.
- Design a new Canadian flag.
- Design a castle.

Other

- Draw a scene from another planet.
- Draw a giant looking down at a village.
- Draw a new creature.
- Draw an alien.
- Draw an airplane.
- Draw a spaceship.
- Draw what you see outside your bedroom window.
- Draw a boat.
- Draw what the world looked like during the time of the dinosaurs.
- Draw a bug.
- Draw a snowman.
- Draw a robot.
- Draw a bird.
- Draw a train.
- Draw a bike.
- Draw and colour a postcard.

Collage

- Summer pictures
- Fall pictures
- Winter pictures
- All about me
- Favourite food
- Favourite colour
- City pictures
- Farm pictures
- Pet pictures
- Animal pictures

Fall Activity Ideas

- Paint a fall mural on the classroom windows using a mixture of equal parts dishwashing liquid and paint (use washable liquid paint or powdered tempera paint). Encourage students to add as many details as possible.

- Make paper ears of corn. Students cut long ear-of-corn shapes from yellow construction paper. Instruct students to glue down small squares of yellow, orange and brown tissue paper to represent the kernels. When the glue is dry, add brown construction paper in the shape of the husk to the back.

- Use orange fingerpaint to make thumbprint pumpkins. Model for students how to press their thumb into the paint and then onto paper. They can fill the page with thumbprints. Once the paint is dry, students can add faces, stems and lines to their pumpkins.

- Make leaf collages. Students should bring in fall leaves in all shapes and sizes, arrange them on a piece of paper, and paste them down.

- Cut out three cups from a cardboard egg carton and show students how to turn them into a bat. First, model for students how to carefully cut out part of the bottoms of the two outside cups. These will be the bat wings. Student can paint the cups black and draw a face.

- Use the shape outline cutouts in this resource to assemble shape pictures of a Halloween cat, witch, haunted house or bat. Students can paint the shapes using a textured paint and glue them onto black construction paper.

- Assemble pasta skeletons. Provide students with different-shaped pieces of pasta and black construction paper. Students should glue the pasta pieces down once they are pleased with their arrangement.

- Create Christmas ornaments using self-hardening clay. Students can use Christmas-themed cookie cutters to form the ornaments. They can use paint, glitter and other materials to decorate them.

- Make festive wrapping paper. Give each student a large piece of white paper. Students can sponge paint Christmas colours and glue on glitter.

- Construct three-dimensional Christmas trees. First, show students how to fold two rectangular pieces of green construction paper in half. Then, draw half a Christmas tree opposite the fold on one piece of paper, place the folded pieces of paper one on top of the other, and cut along the outline to produce two identical, symmetrical tree shapes. Cut a slit along the crease in the centre of the bottom half of one tree and the top half of the other tree. Fit the two shapes together.

- Use the paper doll outlines in this resource to make a scarecrow, witch, Santa, elf, angel, or child. Students can use construction paper to make clothes, yarn for hair, and other found materials.

Winter Activity Ideas

- Paint a winter mural on the classroom windows using a mixture of equal parts dishwashing liquid and paint (use washable liquid paint or powdered tempera paint).

- Use tempera paint to create a winter scene that includes trees and hills. Glue on cotton balls to represent snow.

- Make Valentine's Day pendants using self-hardening clay. Students can mould their own shape or use cookie cutters as guides. Paint the pendants with acrylic paint once the clay is dry.

- Assemble heart cutouts into pictures. Students cut heart shapes of different sizes out of pink, purple and red construction paper. They arrange and glue the hearts to form different animals, such as a mouse, dog, cat, butterfly, or fish. Make extra materials available so students can add eyes, a nose, whiskers, or other details.

- Weave a paper heart. Model for students how to fold a piece of red or pink construction paper exactly in half. Then, using a pencil, draw the outline of half a heart opposite the fold and cut along the outline to create a heart shape. Demonstrate for students how to carefully cut long slits parallel to the fold without cutting the heart into pieces. Then show them how to weave strips of white, red and pink paper through the heart.

- Create a heart crown for Valentine's Day. Students cut heart shapes in different sizes and sponge paint them in different tints and shades of red. Once the hearts are dry, students paste them onto a strip of red construction paper. Staple the strip to fit each student's head. Students could also add glitter to their crowns.

- Construct cute leprechauns for St. Patrick's Day. First, students paint toilet paper tubes green. Once the paint is dry, model for students how to trace the end of the tube onto green paper. Draw a bigger circle around the tracing and cut out the bigger circle. Cut out the smaller circle you traced to form a doughnut shape. Help students slide the doughnut shape over the top of the toilet paper tube to create a leprechaun hat. Students glue on an oval for the face and add facial features. They can glue on short pieces of yarn to form a beard. Lastly, add two rectangles for the leprechaun's arms.

- Go outside on a snowy day and create snow sculptures!

- Dress a paper doll in winter clothes. Students can use the outlines in this resource.

- Make a snowman using self-hardening dough. Students can add branches for arms. Once the dough has hardened, students paint and decorate it with various media.

Spring Activity Ideas

- Paint a spring mural on the classroom windows using a mixture of equal parts dishwashing liquid and paint (use washable liquid paint or powdered tempera paint).

- Create beautiful macaroni necklaces for Mother's Day. Prepare a variety of tube-shaped macaroni in different colours by mixing two to three tablespoons of rubbing alcohol with a few drops of liquid food colouring in a plastic bag. Shake the bag to be sure that the liquid coats all of the macaroni. Let the macaroni dry thoroughly on paper towels. Repeat the process for as many colours as desired. Then, for each necklace give students a length of yarn with one end wrapped tightly with tape. Tie a knot for students at the other end so that the macaroni does not fall off once strung. Encourage students to create a pattern as they construct their necklace. Tie the ends of the necklace together when complete.

- Create a beautiful lily bouquet. Students trace each of their hands onto colourful construction paper and then cut out the shapes. Model for students how to curl each of the fingers of the hand cutout around a pencil. Next, demonstrate how to take the palm of the hand cutout to form a cone with the fingers curling outward. This is the lily. Tape the cone together and then tape it onto a straw (the straw is the stem). Students can make some green leaves to staple onto the stem. Repeat the process so that each student has a lily bouquet.

- Construct a handprint rainbow. Students trace their hands on rainbow-coloured paper (red, orange, yellow, green, blue and purple) and cut out the handprints. Collect the handprints and post them in the shape of a rainbow.

- Use the shape outline cutouts in this resource to create an Easter bunny. Use ovals for ears, small squares for teeth, hearts for feet, overlapping circles for the face and body, and white cotton for the tail. Students paste the bunny onto a construction paper background and use the torn-paper technique to add grass, the sun and other details.

- Decorate paper Easter eggs. Students cut egg shapes out of construction paper and draw line patterns on them with water-based markers. Students can trace over the marker lines with white glue to produce an embossed effect (the glue will dry clear).

- Produce beautiful insect and flower "stained glass" windows using black construction paper and tissue paper. Students cut out the desired shapes from the black construction paper, leaving the "window frame." Then students carefully paste different colours of tissue paper to create a stained glass effect.

- Make a caterpillar using six cups from an egg carton. Students paint the cups green and then add decorations. They can colour in eyes and a mouth and glue on paper antennae.

- Make colourful paper-bag birds. Students start by cutting feathers of different shapes and sizes from construction paper. Demonstrate how to place and glue the feathers around the bag, starting from the back. Encourage students to create a pattern of colour. Students can add triangle-shaped wings covered in feathers, eyes and a beak.

- Design an Earth Day poster.

- Dress a paper doll in a raincoat, rubber boots and hat. Students can use the outlines in this resource.

Summer Activity Ideas

- Paint a summer mural on the classroom windows using a mixture of equal parts dishwashing liquid and paint (use washable liquid paint or powdered tempera paint).

- Make miniature kites. Use straws or wooden craft sticks to construct the frame and cover it with tissue paper. Attach string.

- Create beautiful tissue paper flowers. Students take four to six rectangular pieces of tissue paper and fold them as a pile into an accordion. Next, they tie the centre of the pile with a twist tie. Demonstrate for students how to carefully pull each piece of tissue paper up toward the centre of the flower, so that the pieces of tissue paper are separated to form petals. Finally, add a stem using a green pipe cleaner or Bristol board.

- Celebrate Canada Day. Design a stamp and/or create a diorama depicting all things Canadian.

- Turn a rock into a paperweight and give it as a gift for Father's Day. Invite students to bring rocks to class and to decorate the rock of their choice with acrylic paint.

- Make colourful paper-bag fish. Students start by cutting hearts of different sizes and colours from construction paper. These will be the scales. Demonstrate how to place and glue the scales around the bag. Encourage students to create a pattern of colour. Students can add triangle-shaped fins, a heart-shaped tail and construction-paper eyes.

- Build a sandcastle using sand clay. Once the sandcastle is finished, students should gently pat dry sand on the moist clay.

- Create a diorama of a summer garden or a beach scene.

- Design and create a mixed-media poster of the ultimate vacation spot. Students can use magazine pictures of places they would like to visit for inspiration and reference.

- Use tracings and cutouts to make flowers. Students trace their hands and cut the tracing out the create a flower. They add cutouts (see the shape outline blackline masters in this resource) to form a stem and leaves. Students can paste all the shapes onto a coloured piece of construction paper and fill in each shape with a textured paint.

- Dress a paper doll in beachwear.

- Create sunny sunflowers using shape outlines. Use long ovals for the petals, a circle for the sunflower centre and narrow rectangles for the stem. Either use coloured construction paper or paint the shapes. Students should arrange the shapes on a piece of paper and glue them down. Students can also glue seeds in the centre of the sunflower.

- Draw and colour a picture of a favourite time from the school year.

Fall Colouring Fun

1. Colour and then cut out the fall activity pictures.
2. Paste the pictures onto a separate piece of paper with a fall background that includes trees with leaves that have fall colours.

Winter Colouring Fun

1. Colour and then cut out the winter pictures.
2. Paste the pictures onto a separate piece of paper with a winter background that includes trees and hills.

Spring Colouring Fun

1. Colour and then cut out the spring activity pictures.
2. Paste the pictures onto a separate piece of paper with a spring background that includes a garden with spring flowers.

Summer Colouring Fun

1. Colour and then cut out the summer activity pictures.
2. Paste the pictures onto a separate piece of paper with a summer background that includes a beach and water.

UNDERSTANDING OF ART CONCEPTS RUBRIC

LEVEL	DESCRIPTORS
4	Student shows a thorough understanding of all or almost all concepts and consistently gives appropriate and complete explanations independently. No teacher support is needed.
3	Student shows a good understanding of most concepts and usually gives complete or nearly complete explanations. Infrequent teacher support is needed.
2	Student shows a satisfactory understanding of most concepts and sometimes gives appropriate, but incomplete, explanations. Teacher support is sometimes needed.
1	Student shows little understanding of concepts and rarely gives complete explanations. Intensive teacher support is needed.

COMMUNICATION OF CONCEPTS RUBRIC

LEVEL	DESCRIPTORS
4	Student almost always uses correct art terminology with clarity and precision during class discussions.
3	Student frequently uses correct art terminology during class discussions.
2	Student occasionally uses correct art terminology during class discussions.
1	Student rarely uses correct art terminology during class discussions.

Art Rubrics

CREATIVE WORK RUBRIC

LEVEL	DESCRIPTORS
4	Student applies almost all of the skills, techniques and art concepts taught.
3	Student applies most of the skills, techniques and art concepts taught.
2	Student applies more than half of the skills, techniques and art concepts taught.
1	Student applies fewer than half of the skills, techniques and art concepts taught.

PARTICIPATION RUBRIC

LEVEL	DESCRIPTORS
4	Student consistently contributes to class discussions and activities by offering ideas and asking questions.
3	Student usually contributes to class discussions and activities by offering ideas and asking questions.
2	Student sometimes contributes to class discussions and activities by offering ideas and asking questions.
1	Student rarely contributes to class discussions and activities by offering ideas and asking questions.

Class Evaluation List

Student Name	Class Participation	Understanding of Concepts	Communication of Concepts	Creative Work	Overall Evaluation

Art Websites for Students

Hello Kids

http://www.hellokids.com

Have students visit the "Drawing" section of this fantastic site. Here students will find several easy-to-follow, step-by-step instructions for drawing a variety of animals and characters.

Destination Modern Art

http://www.moma.org/interactives/destination

This fun interactive activity from the Museum of Modern Art is designed for children ages five to eight. An alien creature guides students through various creative and learning activities.

McMichael Canadian Art Collection

http://www.mcmichael.com

This important Canadian gallery houses a permanent collection of almost 6000 artworks by Tom Thomson, the Group of Seven and their contemporaries, as well as First Nations, Inuit and other artists who have made a contribution to Canada's artistic heritage. Teachers and students can view and research objects in the collection online.

Artists in Canada

http://www.artistsincanada.com

A comprehensive national directory of Canadian artists, art galleries and art resources.

The National Gallery of Canada

http://www.gallery.ca

Click on "Learn" to view online exhibitions and to access special interactive features for kids and teens. Themed lesson plans are also available in this part of the website. Each lesson plan includes activities for students at different grade levels.

Build Your Wild Self

http://buildyourwildself.com

This is a great website where students can design a digital human and add a variety of animal characteristics.

Abstract art: Art that uses lines, shapes, colours and textures to portray a realistic object in a non-realistic, imaginary way.

Allegory: The use of symbolic figures to represent abstract ideas such as honour and sacrifice.

Analogous colours: Two or more colours that are next to each other on the colour wheel. For example: red, red-orange and orange.

Background: The part of the picture plane that seems to be farthest from the viewer.

Balance: A principle of design that deals with arranging the visual elements in a work of art for harmony of design and proportion.

Cast shadow: The shadow created on a surface when an objects blocks the light.

Complementary colours: Colours opposite each other on the colour wheel. For example: yellow and purple.

Collage: Creating a picture by gluing pieces of materials such as paper, photos, magazine clippings or found objects to a flat surface.

Colour: Colour is an element of design. Eyes see colour when light bounces off an object. The four characteristics of colour are hue, saturation, value and temperature.

Colour wheel: A tool for creating and organizing colours and representing relationships among colours.

Comic: A graphic art form in which images and words are used to tell a story. The images are the main focus and are usually presented in strip or page layout.

Composition: Describes the organization of the elements of design used in an artwork.

Contemporary art: Art created by living artists.

Contour drawing: An outline drawing that characterizes the edge of a form. In "blind" contour drawing, an artist slowly draws each curve on the edges of an object without looking at the paper.

Contour lines: Lines that define the edges, ridges or outline of a shape or form.

Contrast: A principle of design where light colours are used next to dark colours.

Cool colours: These are the colours that seem to retreat into the background or distance such as green, blue and purple. Colours often associated with cool places, things or feelings.

Elements of design: Colour, line, texture, shape and form.

Focal point: The area in an artwork that attracts the viewer's eye as the centre of interest.

Foreground: The part of the picture plane which appears closest to the viewer and in front of other objects. The foreground is often at the bottom of a picture.

Form: An element of design describing a three-dimensional object.

Foreshortening: A technique used in perspective to produce the illusion of an object retreating into the background.

Horizon line: A level line where water or land seems to end and the sky begins.

Hue: Another word for colour.

Line: An element of design that is used to define shape, contours and outlines. Different lines can suggest a variety of ideas, movements and moods.

Logo: A visual symbol that identifies a business, club, individual or group.

Middle ground: The part of a picture that seems to be in the middle of the picture plane.

Mixed media: Any artwork which uses more than one medium.

Monochromatic: Made using different shades and tints of one colour.

Organic shape: Non-geometric or free-flowing shape.

Perspective: The technique used to represent a three-dimensional world (what we see) on a two-dimensional surface (a piece of paper or canvas) in a way that looks realistic. Perspective is used to generate an illusion of space and depth on a flat surface

Pattern: Lines, colours or shapes repeated in a planned way.

Pointillism: A technique of painting, commonly attributed to Georges Seurat, in which tiny dots of colour are placed close together. From a distance, the dots seem to disappear and the colours blend.

Art Glossary

Primary colours: The basic colours—red, blue and yellow—from which all other colours can be mixed.

Secondary colours: The colours produced by mixing equal amounts of any two primary colours: blue and red produce purple, yellow and red make orange, and blue and yellow make green.

Sgraffito: A technique created by scratching into paint to reveal the colours underneath.

Shade: Dark value of a colour made by adding black.

Shape: An element of design describing the outer form or outline of an image created using line, value, colour and/or texture. Shapes may be geometric or organic, positive or negative.

Sketch: A quick drawing that is used as a reference or plan for an artwork.

Space: An element of design that describes the area around, within or between images or other elements of design.

Still life: An artwork depicting a grouping of inanimate objects.

Subject: A topic or idea represented in an artwork.

Symmetry: Symmetry is demonstrated when portions of the object on opposite sides of a line of symmetry are mirror images one of the other.

Tertiary colours: Colours produced by mixing primary colours with secondary colours.

Tint: Light value of a colour made by adding white.

Texture: An element of design describing the surface quality of an object.

Wash: Created by adding water to paint, making it thin enough to allow colours applied underneath to show through.

Warm colours: Warm colours are used to make an object seem to advance into the foreground. Red, yellow and orange are warm colours. They suggest warm places, things and feelings.

Value: The lightness or darkness of a colour.

Vanishing point: In linear perspective, a position on the horizon where lines or rays between near and distant places appear to come together.

SUPER ARTIST

Keep it up!

ARTIST SUPERSTAR!

GREAT ART!